Faith at Home

The Key Role of the Family in Discipleship (Part 1: the UK)

Mark Griffiths
Dean, St Padarn's Institute

Gareth Hillier
Faith in the Family Networker

Lucy Moore
Head of The Growing Faith Foundation

Rachel Turner
Head of Discipleship, Hope Church, Harrogate

GROVE BOOKS LIMITED
RIDLEY HALL RD CAMBRIDGE CB3 9HU

Contents

Note
The main text of this book has been written by Mark Griffiths with input (indicated in chapter 3) from Gareth Hillier, Lucy Moore and Rachel Turner

First Impression January 2024
ISSN 2753-9369
ISBN 978 1 78827 367 1

1 An Idea Whose Time has Come

Introduction

There is a growing realization that church-based teaching and programmes (whether in services or groups for different ages) alone are inadequate for growing faith and encouraging discipleship amongst children. The importance of working with and within families, encouraging good practices of discipleship as a whole family together, is now seen as key to the passing on of faith to the next generation.

This booklet has its origins in the Anglican Communion group for Intentional Discipleship and, although all the contributors wrote for that context, this is not a distinctly Anglican focus. There are emerging initiatives from Baptists, Methodists, Presbyterians, Pentecostals and many others, all focusing heavily on this ministry area. What the ministries included here have is a reputation as significant ministries operating across the United Kingdom—and many of them have been well received around the world. *Messy Church*, for instance, already has an international reach.

Aims

This book is not merely a list of resources. What we aim to do is provide a list of resourcing organizations with comments on their approach. We also provide some of their theological underpinning in order to make it easier for you to head to the most appropriate resources to use in your situation.

The initiatives this book reflects on are fundamentally UK-based. There is a wonderful tapestry of organizations around the world that are committed to helping families pass on faith within the home. That is why we were keen to call this book 'Part 1.' Our companion volume will complete this exercise with the international perspective. That there are so many organizations focusing in this area shows just how much this is an idea whose time has come. Here are just a few of the ministries we will be exploring:

- *Raising Kids Who Care* (Australia): *'Changing the world, one family at a time'* with themed and structured conversations.
- *Families in Ministry* (Germany): a specialist focus on families in ministry.

- *The Families Course* (New Zealand): part of *Fusion Australia*'s suite of training courses.
- *YWAM Family Ministries International* (worldwide): committed to discipling families using biblical principles for life and relationships.
- *Growing Faith* (Australia): a ministry of *Youthworks Media* that offers wisdom and encouragement for raising Christian children in the modern world.
- *Family Impact* (Africa): providing grassroot support for families nationwide and implementing grassroot support.
- *Family First* (United States): *'Helping Families Love Well. When you give, you'll help provide families with the resources they need to love one another well.'*
- *e625* (South America): the Family Resources Network focuses on helping families better communicate faith across South America.
- *Global Family Challenge* (worldwide): *'Do Home!'* churchwide conversations initiative.
- *Children's Ministry Basics* (Canada): a new website developed by *Scripture Union Canada,* filled with articles, resources, strategies and more for ministry with children and families.

And it is not just para-church organizations that have realized the time has come for a specific focus on supporting Christian parents in passing on their faith to their children. The Church of England is just one example of an institution that has recognized the need to resource families. The *Growing Faith* initiative emanates from the vision outlined by the House of Bishops and ratified by the General Synod in 2019. It could be argued that there should have been an earlier response. As we entered the twentieth century 85% of children were connected to church or Sunday School. As we entered the twenty-first century that number was less than 5%. The story of the twentieth century has been one of freefall in terms of church attendance by young families and their children and teenagers. Bob Jackson writes:

> The decline shown by the Usual Sunday Attendance figures in the number of children (defined as under 16s) attending church in the 1990s was double that of adults.[1] Between one in three and one in four children disappeared from Sunday church between 1990 and 2000. This decline has been going on for so long that there are now also far fewer young adults in church life. For every 100 children in Church of England churches in 1930 today there are nine.[2]

A response was needed and so collaboratively engaging churches, schools and households, *Growing Faith* strives to facilitate a comprehensive approach that empowers children, young people and families to experience the fullness of life. To paraphrase the *Growing Faith* website—the initiative is a movement dedicated to repositioning children, young people and families as the focal point of the church's mission and ministry, thereby effecting a cultural shift within the Church of England, a denomination where it had been estimated that less than a decade earlier, one in four of its churches had no children in attendance at any of its services.

At *Growing Faith*'s core is the advancement of the well-being of children and young people, fostering their agency in shaping the world they aspire to inhabit, particularly through the prism of the Christian faith. To carry forward the *Growing Faith* mission at the local level, each diocese has appointed one or more *Growing Faith* Champions, charged with advancing the initiative within their respective communities.

This is simply how one denomination is approaching the subject. Why not explore what your own church stream is doing? But before looking at specific resources and saying why we think they are important we want to lay out the more fundamental principle—that the centrality of sharing faith across the generations is hardly a new idea. It goes back to the earliest days of our faith.

2 The Judaeo/Christian Perspective

'Faith at home' is only part of the package needed to encourage children and young people in their faith. To gain a more holistic understanding of this will involve a short engagement with family ministry from an historic perspective.[3]

Phil Cliff concluded his PhD on the Sunday School movement with the words, '*Sunday School teachers cannot do for parents what they must do for themselves. The classroom is no substitute for the family.*'[4] Most would certainly agree. But his statement needs further analysis. If we dig a little deeper into this word 'family' we will quickly discover that there are at least two Hebrew words that are translated into the English word 'family.' And a closer inspection quickly reveals that there are interesting nuances that give us some insight.

The first Hebrew word translated family in the Bible is the word *bayit*. *Bayit* means 'house' or 'dwelling' and was used to refer to a family together under one roof. We encounter this word in the instructions for the Passover meal (Exod 12.21–28). On the very first Passover, a lamb was sacrificed and the blood of that lamb placed on the doorpost of individual homes. Inside those homes, the lamb became a family meal celebrated gathered together around the table. This first Passover was the night of liberation, of freedom, and God instructed them to continue to celebrate this meal every year to remember what God had done.

So, every year for thousands of years, Jews have sat down together and celebrated Passover. It is a liturgical ceremony because at the appointed time during the meal the youngest child stands and asks, 'What makes this night special?' This allows the father or mother to make their response by explaining the story of the Passover and of the Exodus. This emphasizes that they serve an active God, but not just a God who *did* things, but a God who *is doing* things today, a God endowed with potentiality—God was active in the past, is active now and will be active in the future.

Faith at home must be about the communication of the active God

Let us not move past this too quickly. Faith at home must be about the communication of the active God. The God who does things. The God who answers prayers. And I am not for a second suggesting this is easy. In my own family we were often caught with the dilemma of whether we shared with our children difficulties we were facing (*eg* financial or emotional or simply the stress of ministry). If we would not involve them in praying our way out of the crisis then, when the miracle happened—and it always happened, God always came through (although it felt that he was never in a rush!)—we could not celebrate the miracle with our children because we had not shared the difficulty in the first place. Of course there is a slight nonsense there—the fact that we had not shared the difficulty did not mean our children did not know; they always did! But the principle is clear enough, if we involve our children in some of our difficulties, they get to see the miracle, they get to see the God who is active in the lives of their parent(s) and can be active in theirs too.

The earliest followers of Jesus continued this practice of communicating the active God, but these stories would be added to. Not only would the account of the Passover and Exodus be recounted, but now also the stories of the Son of God, Jesus who became flesh, who walked on water, fed thousands, healed the sick, raised the dead, was crucified and resurrected. The *bayit* context remains the same, the principle of the communication of an active God remains the same, but the stories change. And added to those stories are personal accounts of how God helped this and that specific family in each generation.

Today across the planet followers of Jesus gather in the context of *bayit* and exchange stories—stories of the Passover and Exodus, stories of incarnation and resurrection, and new stories of the God who heals, empowers his church and does miracles. It is really important to recognize how long faith in the home has been vital to the passing on of that faith.

But it is also important to note that *bayit* is not the word most commonly translated 'family' in the Old Testament. That honour goes to *mishpachah*. This word connotes a wider connection—clan or community; it is in effect a bond of kinship uniting people to a common cause. Deuteronomy 6.5–7 and Deut 11.18–19, when instructions are given for the passing on of the belief system from one generation to the next, are written in the context of *mishpachah*.

That which constitutes a family in the Old Testament is the bond of kinship that unites its members; *mishpachah* includes all those to whom that kinship extends. So when a Hebrew boy reached the age of marriage he would travel to the home of his wife to be and propose (weddings were usually arranged by the parents, so his proposal was a sure thing!). Once she had formally accepted and hung the lit lantern in her window to indicate that she was now engaged, the young Hebrew man would return and begin construction of a new set of rooms added onto his family home, or a new house next door. When this was completed, the bride would move to her new

That which constitutes a family is the bond of kinship that unites its members

home (via a week of celebrations). Other sons within the same house would be doing a similar thing and in turn the son's sons would follow the pattern. Over time, what started out as a family would become an extended family, a further extended family and eventually a whole tribe (Hebrew archaeology supports this, with archaeological digs often revealing a central older residence and newer residences emanating out from there). *Mishpachah* is the word used to describe this group of people (that could number thousands). And every member of this *mishpachah* recognized their responsibility to communicate the faith of their *mishpachah* to the children of that group.

This pattern was continued by the early followers of Jesus. When they gathered in Solomon's Colonnade there would have been children present, and all the members of this new Jesus community recognized their responsibility to communicate the Jesus story into the lives of the children of this newly formed Jesus *mishpachah* (Acts 5.12).

And of course, while the *bayit* looks like our modern families, *mishpachah* looks like church—not the building but the community, a gathering of people united together with a common cause. And in the same way that all the members of the original *mishpachah* recognized their responsibility to communicate the faith to the new generation, so should the members of our congregations. But it is slightly subtler than that. The Jewish understanding is that the whole community *do* communicate. Whether they choose to or not. Not just the children's team! *All the members communicate*. Our attitudes, our passions, our commitments, the way we worship, the way we respond to others, all communicate to the children of our *mishpachah*.

To belong to a mishpachah is a privilege that comes with responsibility

To belong to *mishpachah* is a privilege, but it is a privilege that comes with responsibility. When was the last time you heard someone preach this message—'To be part of this church community is a privilege, but it is a privilege that comes with responsibility'? Freedom in Christ means we have liberty to say what we want—but that does not mean saying all that we might want to! We are responsible for our attitudes in front of that rising generation.

The Jewish heritage in the form of both *bayit* and *mishpachah* has the power to transform twenty-first-century practice in a Christian context. Both are of fundamental importance. It is though *bayit* where our focus lies for this book. And it is so important. According to the 21st Century Evangelicals Survey undertaken by the Evangelical Alliance, 54% of the present UK church cited growing up in a Christian home as the primary reason they are in church today. That is in contrast to 6% citing a course as their way in. The obvious reality is that faith in the home is a significant factor in future church attendance.

However, one in every two children growing up in a Christian home do not go on to become adult worshippers.[5] One further statistic may go some way to explain this; only 31% of those who said their faith was important to them felt it especially important to pass on to their children in the home.[6]

Passing on faith in the home is of central importance and we will return to this as our focus shortly. But it is not enough. If all we are doing is passing on faith within our existing Christian homes and Christian churches, we have a problem. Most homes across the UK right now are at least four generations removed from the Jesus story; children do not know Jesus, parents do not know Jesus, grandparents do not know Jesus, great grandparents do not know Jesus.[7] Scripture Union records that only 5% of English churches have any children in them. It is just 3% in Wales.

Why is passing on faith in the home seen as unimportant by so many? Whatever the reason, there is clearly work to be done in this area. How might we do both things together, pass faith on in the home and also tell non-Christians about Jesus?

We have an increasing number of first-generation followers of Jesus in our churches (which is good news, it means we are doing evangelism), but this may mean that they were not brought up in an environment where faith was important and therefore they do not know how to pass on their faith.[8] And sometimes, worse still ,there is an assumption by the new convert that they came to faith in their 30s and 40s and maybe their children will do the same. So faith at home resources are going to need to stretch to discipling our new Christians who happen to be parents in how to disciple their own children. The writer of Proverbs was keen to point out that training up children in the way they should go is important and the principle still holds true.

First-generation followers of Jesus do not know how to pass on their faith

I offer these thoughts from a position of experience. I came to faith aged 15 from a home where nobody had ever been to church. My wife came from a nominally Christian context in that her mother went to church on Sundays. But faith at home was not a thing. So, when our first child was born, where were we to draw our pattern of parenting from? We did not have one. We had to learn. Prayers over our children when they are poorly, prayers before eating meals, prayers when facing crucial life events—going to school / university / work for the first time. Bible stories at bedtime. All things we had to learn. But there was nobody helping us. The assumption was that we would know how to pass on the faith. Today we have many wonderful organizations and exceptional resources to equip parents to do the work of discipling their children. I would suggest this is so important that we should build on to our *Alpha/Emmaus/Christian Enquirer* courses a few sessions on just why it is important to communicate faith within the home and, almost more importantly, how we pass on that faith.

Child evangelism must be part of the equation. We need to find ways to communicate the Jesus story to children and young people who would never hear that story within their home, primarily because their parents and grandparents do not have faith. So, across our world we also need to give profile to those ministries whose calling is to see children and young people from non-Christian homes come to faith. Of course that is complex. But it is also necessary. And it is a personal plea, because without the efforts of the girl who invited me to come to church when I was 15 it is likely that I would not be a follower of Jesus today. That is why we also plan to add a booklet on child evangelism to this series.

It is not an either / or. Evangelism in general and child evangelism in particular should not be neglected in our desire to do family ministry well. Allow me to explain it this way. John is 7 and lives down the road from your church. He comes to your midweek club and really enjoys it. When he first came, he did not know the songs, and did not quite know what to make of the stories and games, but he liked it, especially the prizes! His parents do not come to your church. They visit at Christmas, but that is it. John, though, comes every week.

Susie, 6, comes to the same club reluctantly. She lives with her mum, a single parent who sends Susie to the kid's club to get some time to herself. Susie resents being sent, but six months in she is over the resentment, and she is also enjoying it. Her mum never attends; she uses the phrase, 'it's not for me.'

John and Susie come faithfully. They move into the youth group and become part of the Sunday congregation. When John and Susie turn 25 they decide they like each other and several years later marry and have children of their own. The question is, how did your church connect with John and Susie? Child evangelism—you communicated Jesus to a boy and a girl who would never hear that story any other way. But what about John and Susie's children? Well, they belong to an entire community who have their responsibility to communicate faith to them. And John and Susie in the context of their family, their *bayit,* will communicate faith to their children. This is both exciting and effective. This pattern of faith communicated in the home takes three generations to break (grandparents / parents / children do not have faith) but only one generation to fix. It just needs enough churches to get a vision for connecting and communicating to children who are not currently part of a church or church group.

Our focus is on the transmission of faith from one generation to the next in the context of the home. It is important that we do this well. It was not difficult to identify the three primary activities / ministries that are engaging with this area across Ireland and the UK. They bubbled to the surface quite naturally as they have significant users and prominence, and this engagement grows week on week. We will use three case studies for this booklet:

- *Messy Church* (and *Messy Church at Home*)
- The *Kitchen Table Project*
- *Parenting for Faith*

On face value, *Parenting for Faith* and the *Kitchen Table Project* appear far more focused on equipping parents to communicate faith to their children in the context of the home, and *Messy Church* appears to be more of an activity for parents to attend with their children. But *Messy Church* is more than simply an activity afternoon for families, as will be explained. These three initiatives are explored in the next chapter. Following further reflections, there is a resources section at the end to show the range of help available

3 Three Examples

Messy Church (Lucy Moore)

Messy Church is an international phenomenon, with around 1600 registered churches across more than 30 countries and most mainstream denominations. It is a way of being church for families and others, which enables people to encounter Jesus in a relaxed space in their local church. *Messy Church* is Christ-centred, for all ages, and involves creativity, hospitality and celebration (its five core values). It is primarily aimed at people who do not already belong to another form of church and the usual point of entry is one or more adults accompanied by one or more children. It is supported by BRF (Bible Reading Fellowship) Ministries.

Messy Church is Christ-centred, for all ages, and involves creativity, hospitality and celebration

Although in initial concept a once-a-month activity there are now many weekly *Messy Church* gatherings. A session typically includes a welcome, a long creative time to explore the biblical theme through hands-on activities; a short celebration time involving story, prayer, song, games and similar; and a sit-down meal together at tables.

It tries to be as appealing to adults as to children in all its aspects. There is an emphasis on engagement and participation, on enjoyment (celebration is, after all, a core value) and an unwritten invitation to come just as you are in your messy relationships, with your imperfectly-behaved family members and your doubts, questions, lack of interest in Christian spirituality—to bring your messy life to Jesus and his equally *Messy Church* family. The unconditional welcome and abundant generosity (a plethora of lovely activities, a service short enough to be acceptable to the bounciest toddler, a hot meal) attract people who are often right at the start of their faith journey, so any measure of discipleship includes a very generous understanding of a journey with Jesus that may begin a long way before we even notice we are on it. It is also an example of a communal discipleship, with a family group walking together rather than simply an individualistic experience.

The two main aspects of discipleship are that of the adults and children who belong to the *Messy Church* growing in faith together through a shared family experience within the wider family of the local church and the discipleship of the team members who are usually lay people with no recognized authority or licence. The opportunities to grow in missional understanding, to develop leadership skills, take responsibility for evangelism and witness, serving, prayer, biblical interpretation and leading worship are valuable.

There have been some wonderful examples of *Messy Church* when it reaches a more developed form. A *Messy Church* in Birmingham formed in 2013 now operates every Sunday afternoon and will typically see 100 to 150 people attend. The leaders freely acknowledge that it is a challenge because of the scale of the resourcing it requires. But they also emphasize that the amount of work necessarily meant that those who initially attended soon got involved in running activities, helping with food and possibly the most difficult task—cleaning up afterwards. It allowed people to move from attenders to contributors very quickly.

The scale also meant that creative ways had to be found to help disciple people in smaller groups. So weekly small groups emerged from the initial *Messy Church*, with the core values of *Messy Church* remaining key. This *Messy Church* also sees regular baptisms as part of the Sunday afternoon gathering.

Few *Messy Churches* are this big in terms of attendance, but this in itself gives opportunity. There is no need to establish a series of small sub-groups. Discipleship becomes a clear and manageable goal in the whole.

And what is interesting in *Messy Church*, as indeed with all the projects considered here, is that they see the activities not as running an event. They all see their purpose as making disciples. It might be considered that *Messy Church* is possibly more focused on *mishpachah* than *bayit*, however. It is offered here because of the emphasis on whole families learning and worshipping together.

Kitchen Table Project (Gareth Hillier)

Care for the Family developed the *Kitchen Table Project* in response to research showing that many Christian parents struggle to know how to nurture their children's faith. Instead of feeling confident to build faith at home, parents relied heavily on their church and expert nature of children's ministry.

Many Christian parents struggle to know how to nurture their children's faith

The project aims to help parents and carers see that they are the most important influence on their children—on average, it would take a children's worker 421 years of weekly contact to reach the same amount of time with a child as the parents would have with them before the child was ten.[9] Parents can model what it means to live in relationship with God every day in a way that is hard to achieve in Sunday school or similar. Children's work at church is valuable, but the greatest impact is when children see faith lived out in both the tough times and the good times.

The research also revealed that parents did not know where to start—they felt they did not have enough time, that they were not a good enough example, and, above all, they worried about getting it wrong. The *Kitchen Table Project* seeks to help parents overcome those hurdles and encourage parents that sharing their faith with their children is not about adding yet another task to their long to-do list. The key is to be intentional. The project encourages parents to look for opportunities to show their faith in normal, everyday life, finding simple ways to help their children connect with God. This could include when they are walking them to school, over meals, at bedtime, queueing at the supermarket, or waiting for a sibling to come out of school.

Through the project's email newsletters, regular social media posts and other resources parents are given reminders and ideas to help them as they encourage their children's faith to grow. Parents are helped to realize that they are not alone in their journey, that many other parents feel the same as them. The *Kitchen Table Project* small group resources such as *Raising Faith* have been valuable in helping parents to gather together and form communities of support where they can share ideas and encourage each other on their journey.

Of course churches also have a vital role to play in supporting parents—as they begin to see that it is not just about children's work on a Sunday, but about equipping and encouraging parents to feel able to share faith with their children through the week. Through the project's church toolkit, events and small group resources, churches can start to create a culture of becoming parent-equipping churches—recognizing the role parents play in discipling their children in everyday life as a ministry, and helping to build strong intergenerational links, where everyone has a part to play in supporting families and nurturing children's faith.

But *Kitchen Table* has also continued to evolve and now a project called INSPIRE has been added to the programme. A few mums, dads, carers and others get together at someone's home or church. Five-minute video clips help introduce the topic and what the Bible says about faith at home, and the leader's guide gives some questions to help discussions and give opportunity to share experiences—good and ill. Questions such as, 'Why is it important to share our faith with our children at home?' It is another piece of the support package and again helps build strong disciples. Its focus is on helping and equipping parents to be able to share their faith. Built on strong research, *Kitchen Table* has understood that not all parents and carers see the need to pass on faith, and those who do do not find it easy. *Kitchen Table* is an important tool in our toolbox for building stronger families.

Parenting for Faith (Rachel Turner)

Parenting for Faith has been growing since it started in an Anglican church over 15 years ago. Its goal is to equip parents and carers to help their children and teenagers meet and know God and to equip churches to become a culture where faith at home can flourish. Parents and carers do not just need encouragement but envisioning and equipping with skills and tools to help them feel confident to help their children and teens on their faith journey.

For this, *Parenting for Faith* has created a range of free video courses, complete with downloadable leader and participant guides, as well as supplements for leaders to help apply the course to families with children with additional needs. The original course is applicable to all ages and stages and there are also courses that apply this specifically to parents and carers of babies and toddlers; parents who are also church or ministry leaders and parents of teenagers. It produces a weekly podcast covering different topics that families might encounter and equipping them with skills to approach these. Regular Facebook live sessions called 'pop-up small groups' allow *Parenting for Faith* to connect with parents directly on topics seasonal and pressing for them. There are books for parents about spiritual parenting: *Parenting Children for a Life of Faith, Parenting Children for a Life of Purpose* and *Parenting Children for a Life of Confidence,* all included in the new omnibus version of the first title. There are two devotionals for parents to explore with children called *Comfort in the Darkness* and *Comfort in Uncertain Times.*

There are currently 500 searchable articles and videos on *Parenting for Faith.* These are being constantly added to as parents request the topics which are most helpful to them. There is also a range of resources specifically for outreach to parents of babies and toddlers—including slimline books written for families on the fringe of church to give away during baptisms, toddler groups, celebrating the arrival of a new baby, during baby and toddler groups—all to help nurture your child's spiritual life. These books are accompanied by a video curriculum to support toddler groups as well as baptism families, a supplement to help apply the *Parenting for Faith* course to young families and an online conference for churches to explore how to support parents taking their first steps in faith at home.

Parenting for Faith also supports the development of churches wanting to support faith at home. The book *It Takes a Church to Raise a Parent* equips churches in how to empower parents effectively to help their child and teen's faith grow proactively. There is also an online short course enabling leaders to achieve a certificate in *Parenting for Faith.*

The *Parenting for Faith* team learnt early on that for church leaders to support faith at home confidently they themselves need to be supported and encouraged. For this reason, *Parenting for Faith* conducted years of research which led to the book *Parenting as a Church Leader—Helping Your Family Thrive*. This has been accompanied by a series of online training days specifically for church leaders and their unique parenting context.

Conclusion

4

The true success of these projects is difficult to measure in the short term and will only be shown as successful if there are more disciples of Jesus and families become more aware of their responsibility to communicate faith to the next generation in years to come. *Messy Church* has been established longer than the others and therefore it is easier to look at this over a longer time span. It also benefits from a recent independent analysis of its activities by the Church Army which confirmed the effectiveness of *Messy Church* in terms of:[10]

- reaching people who did not previously attend church
- growing disciples
- modelling new patterns of leadership
- and doing so across a wide range of economic and social contexts

However, there is sometimes a pushback against the focus of these projects with a suggestion that some, especially those without children, may feel alienated by the constant emphasis on family. Fortunately there is a growing awareness that this emphasis on families is not about excluding those who do not feel they are part of a family, but rather drawing attention afresh to the biblical understanding of church as family. Loneliness has been termed a twenty-first-century epidemic.[11] Psalm 68.6 tells us that God sets the lonely in families. You would not have to visit too many churches running a Sunday afternoon *Messy Church* to see how quickly those who attend are drawn in and feel part of family. Pop in and ask someone who has only been there for a few weeks; they will articulate this feeling of family well.

That is why activities like *Messy Church* have an extra dimension; they are not just about discipling families, they are also about developing a new generation of leaders. It may be an approach that starts a long way down the Engel Scale but young people acting as junior leaders, serving as apprentices to an older leader is an excellent form of discipleship.[12] And it is a form of discipleship that models so many kingdom values in terms of community, a far more intergenerational model pushing against centuries of church practice where church = adults—a more organic approach, a family approach.

And within this there is the rediscovery of the embedded truth we identified earlier, *mishpachah,* stretching back to the earliest tribe / village, where all the members of the original faith communities recognized their responsibility to communicate faith to the rising generation. We need to be the same today. Our attitudes, our passions, our commitments, the way we worship, the way we respond to others, all communicate to the children of that faith community.

Everyone in a faith community communicates to the children of *that community,* not just the children's team or youth workers. As that slightly unhappy man who sits on the front row and constantly complains that we do not sing enough hymns communicates his frustration into the lives of the children of that community, so too that newly-married couple who know that they maybe should be putting in more overtime at work because they could do with the extra money, but instead choose to miss out on extra income for the sake of choir or worship practice—when they stand in front of the church on Sunday morning they communicate their love and sacrifice to the children of the community. Neither are in the children's or youth team, but that does not matter—everyone who is part of a faith community communicates to the children and young people of the community. As we have said, to belong to a church is a privilege that comes with responsibility—something that needs preaching! We are all responsible for our attitudes in front of that rising generation.

So, we are aiming for parents and carers passing on faith to the next generation, with the wonderful organizations we have explored providing support. Our congregations can provide encouragement, recognizing that they are not consumers but contributors. Our ministers can continually explain and promote the role of the family, giving biblical wisdom that reinforces the fact that we are all in this together and helping to ensure that our families are properly resourced. Faith at home can grow, supported by faith demonstrated in our congregations, with an additional focus on communicating the gospel to those who have never heard the glorious, transformative message of Jesus.

Faith at home can work all over our world

But within the leadership of churches there is still resistance and/or a sense that they are either unaware of the importance and significance of this or simply reluctant to engage with anything looking like intergenerational worship—possibly not having the confidence or training to implement it.[13] Training is a key factor here. Many of our theological colleges provide little (if any) direct training for ministers in working with children, young people and families. As a result one of the keys to church growth is neglected. It rarely makes it onto the agenda for Continuing Ministerial Development days for curates, ministers, pastors either. I have often been an option in the last weeks of the last term of trainee ministers' time at theological college. On the most recent visit those training for ministry were given a choice between attending the session on intergenerational worship run by me or attending the sessions on how to take a funeral. My session did not need the largest room! But it hints at the priorities that we give these things.

Curiously the COVID-19 pandemic had a positive impact on many churches in relation to this. Most congregations developed some sort of online service with many reporting significantly higher attendance than they would see on a typical Sunday before the pandemic. What also quickly emerged was an understanding that churches did not have the ways and means to run a main service with separate provision for children and young people online. Children and young people and parents and single people and older people were all watching the same service, many of them in support bubbles watching on the same screen.[14] Some church leaders recognized that intergenerational worship was the only way to go. People soon discovered that services that were able to communicate to all ages at once were not as difficult as they assumed. And, after all, Jesus did it all the time.[15] *Messy Church, Kitchen Table* and *Parenting for Faith*[16] all went online during that season and were highly effective and able to provide important tools for parents and carers.[17] *Messy Church* adapted even further and became *Messy Church* at Home and developed resources that could be distributed widely, with packs of activities being dropped off at large numbers of homes. Many local churches too sent out home-based resources, from do-it-yourself Christingles to materials to resource a holiday club at home. One group of churches in Lincoln, UK are still doing this, resourcing around 200 families regularly with Bible story related crafts. It looked like family ministry had come of age, all ages together in a weekly service, families resourced through regular *Parenting for Faith* and *Kitchen Table* online seminars and *Messy Church* at Home providing resource and activities. But the end of the pandemic marked a return to the familiar segregated age groups with no longer the perceived need to engage with the community at the same level. It might be an interesting exercise to sit as a church and ask—'What good things were developed during the numerous lockdowns that might still be relevant to us now?'

In the COVID-19 pandemic intergenerational worship was the only way to go

There is one final element that should be considered as part of our conclusion. Does context make a difference? And the answer is of course; all theology is contextual! But there is an assumption beyond contextualization that suggests that these initiatives only work with a certain socio-economic group. Is it easier to implement faith in the home in middle-class suburbs than it is to implement it in council estates? Anecdotal evidence suggests that many of our poorest housing estates have high levels of community connection.[18] But community cohesion alone does not of itself translate into an acceptance of the Christian message or promote faith in the home. However, in those areas of deprivation where *Parenting for Faith* courses have been launched, the take-up is good and the response positive. The Church Army report into *Messy Church* concluded that the initiative was equally effective in areas of social deprivation and in the suburbs.

And there is one other value to these initiatives. It is not just that they are excellent initiatives; there have been many excellent initiatives through the years that have come and gone. Having expressions of discipleship in the context of the home and with families is only part of the process. Historically, the initiatives that have grown and had a transformative impact on the church and helped transform communities are those initiatives that understand the importance of propagation, of communicating good news stories far and wide, both the why and the how, but more importantly the impact on the lives of ordinary people.[19] Visit the *Messy Church, Kitchen Table* or *Parenting for Faith* websites and you will see story after story of lives transformed, of families and communities impacted by the work of these initiatives. Stories can communicate in a way that facts and figures cannot. Explaining to a church leader the need for discipleship in the home, for intergenerational gatherings and intergenerational worship may not be enough to persuade them to try it, but highlighting the fruit of such a ministry may prove effective, particularly if the outcome is more mature members, larger congregations and a more successful integration of church and home.

What is becoming increasingly clear is that the Holy Spirit is breathing on this whole area of intergenerational ministry. The idea has come of age. Faith within families can grow, as seen in the emergence of the above initiatives. Parents are beginning actively to seek ways to equip themselves to disciple their children, and many of our churches are beginning to recognize their role in supporting this, although as previously mentioned church leaders often feel ill equipped. Some of this emphasis came about as a necessity in the pandemic and there is a fear that the gains may well be lost as society moves into a post-COVID-19 era. But this is more than recognizing that the Holy Spirit is breathing on this area. So there must be an emphasis on walking in time with the Spirit.

In terms of outreach to families, Lucy Moore comments that *Messy Church* was created to engage those on the fringe. Now that *Messy Church* has become increasingly central to the main diet of the church, what is being developed to engage with the new fringe?[20] The need to innovate and resource continually in fresh ways is clear. There is a need to ask intentionally, what new resources and initiatives will be needed to support Christian parents as we begin to further understand the necessity and importance of discipleship in the home?

This booklet is written in part with the hope that it will encourage church leaders put families (*bayit* and *mishpachah*) at the centre of their ministry activities, and more—that it will bring forth a whole new generation of initiatives able to meet people at the fringe.

Recommendations for Discussion, Consideration and Further Thought

- A start is to give far more attention to training and equipping ministers to work with children, young people and families.
- A church can communicate at all levels the value of sharing stories and examples of Christian households who are living out their faith at home.
- We can invite our congregations to take an interest in and appropriately support households with children.
- We can discover how to learn from younger members of the church as well as learning with them.
- All ministerial training could include practical experience and reflective time focusing on aspects of ministry that includes children and young people.
- The phrase 'I don't do children' should ring alarm bells in the ministerial selection procedure.
- The default setting for most local ministry could become intergenerational rather than age-segregated.
- We can devise new worship liturgy for an intergenerational context.
- Churches should be encouraged to provide easily accessible training and certification / licensing / commissioning in intergenerational ministry.
- Nothing should be done in age-segregated groups in churches that could be done with all ages together.
- The importance of intergenerational worship should form part of a church leader's core teaching to their congregation.

Indicative Bibliography

M Griffiths, *One Generation from Extinction* (Oxford: Lion, 2009)

M Griffiths, *Changing Lives* (Oxford: Lion, 2017)

L Moore, *Messy Church: Fresh Ideas for Building a Christ-Centered Community* (Westmont, IL: IVP, 2017)

E Powell and C Clark, *Sticky Faith* (Chicago, IL: Zondervan, 2011)

R Turner, *Parenting Children for a Life of Faith Omnibus: Helping Children Meet and Know God* (Oxford: BRF, 2019)

Reports

Church Army, 'Playfully Serious' (Sheffield: Church Army, 2019)

M Griffiths, survey, 'Future First' (Brierly Consultancy, April 2016)

'Talking Jesus' (London: Evangelical Alliance, Church House Publishing, 2015)

D Voas and L Watt, Church growth research (Feb 2014) (online)

O Mark, 'Passing on Faith' (London: Theos, 2016)

Websites

www.eauk.org
www.brf.org.uk
www.careforthefamily.org.uk
www.virtualsundayschooluk.com/
www.24-7prayer.com/resource/lectioforfamilies/
https://churcharmy.org/our-work/research/recently-completed-research/playfully-serious/

Podcasts

https://www.faithinkids.org/podcasts
https://www.churchandculture.org/church-culture-podcast
https://www.bdeducation.org.uk/podcasts/
https://www.parentingforfaith.brf.org.uk/podcast/
https://www.careforthefamily.org.uk/support-for-you/family-life/parent-support/parenting-podcasts/

https://open.spotify.com/episode/6Z9vGTZHe7CzD3eQZxlSOy?si=wAx47lIHTHGZKKPfECeUrQ

Blogs

http://www.childrencan.co.uk/blog/—Leadership, children, spiritual gifts, mission and evangelism
http://flamecreativekids.blogspot.co.uk/—Creative children's ministry

Resources

This list is in no particular order and is undoubtedly not comprehensive, but it does represent the collected wisdom of dozens and dozens of children and family workers who responded to our Facebook requests for resource recommendations. This is their list:

Wisdom and Inspirational Books

B Wilson, *Whose Child Is This?: A Story of Hope and Help for a Generation at Peril* (Brooklyn: Metro Ministries, 2012)

O Goldenberg, *The Josiah Generation: New Dawn, New Rules, New Rulers* (Maidstone: River Publishing and Media Ltd, 2011)

M Griffiths, *One Generation from Extinction* (Oxford: Lion, 2009)

M Griffiths, *Changing Lives* (Oxford: Lion, 2017)

A Shepherd, *Honey, I Blew Up the Kid's Ministry* (Presence Resources, 2007)

J Berryman, *The Spiritual Guidance of Children: Montessori, Godly Play, and the Future* (New York: Morehouse Publishing, 2013)

C Edward, *Slugs and Snails and Puppy Dogs' Tails—Helping Boys Connect with God* (Leicester: IVP, 2011)

I Beckwith, *Formational Children's Ministry: Shaping Children Using Story, Ritual, and Relationship* (Ada, MI: Baker Books, Emergent Village, 2010)

B Lewis, *Raising Children in a Digital Age: Enjoying the Best, Avoiding the Worst* (Oxford: Lion, 2014)

D Csinos and I Beckwith, *Children's Ministry in the Way of Jesus* (Leicester: IVP, 2013)

Y Morris, *Side by Side with God in Everyday Life: Helping Children to Grow with God Through All Times* (Oxford: Barnabas for Children, 2011)

John H Westerhoff, *Will our Children have Faith* (New York: Morehouse Publishing, 2012)

J Berryman, *Godly Play* (series) (Denver, CO: Morehouse Education Resources)

L Moore, *Messy Church* (series) (Oxford: BRF)

Family Specific

R Joiner, *Think Orange: Imagine the Impact When Church and Family Collide* (Colorado Springs, CO: David C Cook, 2009)

L Alexander, *Children, Families and God: Drawing the Generations Together to Change the World* (San Giovanni Teatino: Evangelista Media, 2012)

G Crispin and E Mackenzie, *Together with God: An Introduction to Family Worship* (Birmingham: Morse-Brown Publishing, 2016)

T Preston and T Tolman, Collide—*Exploring Intergenerational Ministry* (Discovery Learning Series, 2013)

R Turner, *Parenting Children for a Life of Faith: Helping Children Meet and Know God* (Oxford: BRF, 2018)

K White, *The Growth of Love: Understanding Five Essential Elements of Child Development* (London: WTL Publications Limited, 2023)

To Help Families

www.godventure.co.uk—books and resources

Treasure boxes from The Treasure People (https://www.facebook.com/thetreasureboxpeople/)

A Buckley, *Play through the Bible* (Epsom: The Good Book Company, 2014)

O Goldenberg, *At Home with God: A Parents' Guide to Raising Spiritual Giants* (London: Children Can, 2019)

Engage Worship: https://engageworship.org/ideas

A Mitchell, *Beginning with God* (series) (Epsom: The Good Book Company)

www.familyministry.co.uk

S and B Legg, *All Together: The Family Devotional* (Farnham, Surrey: CWR, 2017)

Parenting for Faith: www.ParentingForFaith.org

Messy Church: www.messychurch.org

https://littleworshipcompany.com/

The *Kitchen Table* Project: www.kitchentable.org.uk

Home for Good (adoption and fostering): https://www.homeforgood.org.uk

O and H Goldenberg, 50 audio devotionals for families: https://www.ahwg.co.uk/podcast

Kids' Devotionals

S Young, *Jesus Calling: 365 Devotions For Kids* (Nashville, TN: Tommy Nelson Books, 2020)

Children and Spiritual Gifts

Ishmael, *Reclaiming a Generation* (Eastbourne: Kingsway Publications, 200)

Curriculum

M Griffiths and J Foster, *Lightbringers* (Reading: Freedom in Christ, May 2018) (https://www.freedominchrist.org/families)

M Griffiths, *Fusion: A Whole Year's Worth of Teaching Material for 5-12s* (Oxford: Monarch, 2004)

M Griffiths, *Impact: A Whole Year's Worth of Teaching Materials for 5-12s* (Oxford: Monarch, 2003)

M Griffiths, *Detonate: A Whole Year's Worth of Teaching Materials for 5-12s* (Oxford: Monarch, 2005)

Scripture Union, *Rooted* (https://content.scriptureunion.org.uk/rooted)

D Pratt, *7 Gifts for our Children* (http://nnsw.adventist.org.au/family)

Bible Buds (www.biblebuds.co.uk)

Notes

1 Usual Sunday attendance figures are collated by Church of England churches to show average attendance on a given Sunday when there are no festivals or baptisms. An attempt to rationalize the process began from 2000 when churches were asked to record the average of attendance throughout October. The return showed an increase of 10% from the figures presented in 1999—either there are clear difficulties in collating the figures or remarkable church growth took place between 1999 and 2000. It is likely to be the former rather than the latter.

2 Bob Jackson, *Hope for the Church* (London: Church House Publishing, 2002) pp 10-11.

3 The following section is adapted from the book *Changing Lives* by M Griffiths (Oxford: Lion 2017).

4 P Cliff, *The Rise and Development of the Sunday School Movement in England 1780-1980* (London: CEP, 1986).

5 D Voas and L Watt, 'Church Growth Research Programme Report on Numerical Change in Church Attendance: National, Local, and Individual Factors' (February 2014) (https://www.jstor.org/stable/4621936).

6 O Mark, *Passing on Faith* (London, Theos, 2016). This figure was recorded slightly higher at 36% in M Griffiths, 'Future First' (Brierly Research, survey) (April 2016).

7 For more detail on this read M Griffiths, *One Generation from Extinction* (Oxford: Monarch Books, 2009).

8 Statistics taken from M Griffiths, 'Will they have faith?' published in 'Future First,' *op cit* (2016).

9 General Synod Board of Education, 'Children in the Way: New Directions for the Church's Children' (London: The National Society/Church House Publishing, 1989).

10 In a little more detail, this research has discovered:

CELEBRATE · *Messy Church* is reaching families who are new to church · *Messy Church* is growing disciples · *Messy Church* is modelling new patterns of leadership · *Messy Church*es are developing and maturing as church

CHALLENGES exist around how · *Messy Church* leaders are over-stretched and under-supported · *Messy Church*es can find creating a culture of discipleship demanding · *Messy Church*es are often vulnerable and under-resourced · *Messy Church*es live with ambiguity over what it means to be church

MORE has been learned · Being intentional about discipleship is important · Meeting more frequently is not necessarily 'the' answer · Real community is messy

11 K Bakhtiara, 'Gen-Z, The Loneliness Epidemic And The Unifying Power Of Brands,' *Forbes* (2023).

12 The Evangelical Alliance define the Engel Scale in this way, '"The Engel Scale" originates with James F Engel, from the book *What's Gone Wrong with the Harvest?*

published by Zondervan in 1975. The insight into evangelism that is generally drawn from the Engel scale is that all people go on a journey or process on their way to conversion and then on into discipleship.' (https://www.eauk.org/great-commission/what-is-the-engel-scale)

13 The research on what helps young people stay part of church conducted by Fuller Seminary California concluded that, 'There is no golden bullet, but the closest we have is the need for children and young people to see adults worshipping.' (www.fulleryouthinstitute.org)

14 www.gov.uk/guidance/making-a-support-bubble-with-another-household

15 Jesus talked to the oldest old person, the family, the aunties and uncles and all hearing that message of truth in their own way, communicating so well that the child came over and offered his bread and fish (John 6).

16 Youth groups tended to fare less well with young people disconnecting from their online world relatively quickly. When school lessons were being delivered online, and the youth group lacked the physical aspects that young people needed, the addition of an online evening group seemed a step too far. However, the return to in-person groups has been received well by young people.

17 However, it is acknowledged where family situations were toxic, it proved to be a difficult and often dangerous time for some. (https://learning.nspcc.org.uk/research-resources/2020/coronavirus-insight-briefing-domestic-abuse/)

18 Stories coming from the Eden Churches planted by the Message Trust that are deliberately planted into lower socio-economic areas report higher levels of community cohesion.

19 Highlighted spectacularly in the birth of the Sunday School movement in 1780 which went from a small expression in Gloucester to 300,000 children in church and church groups by 1788, achieved primarily by Robert Raikes' (the owner of a newspaper) ability to propagate his product. See M Griffiths, *One Generation from Extinction* (Oxford: Monarch Books, 2009).

20 The majority of all recorded Fresh Expressions in the UK and Ireland are *Messy Church*.